Woman,
YOU ARE

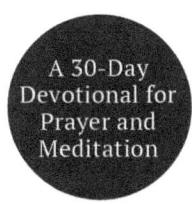

A 30-Day Devotional for Prayer and Meditation

Woman, YOU ARE

Terrah S. Bell

publish
your gift

WOMAN, YOU ARE
Copyright © 2022 Terrah S. Bell
All rights reserved.

Published by Publish Your Gift®
An imprint of Purposely Created Publishing Group, LLC

No part of this book may be reproduced, distributed or transmitted in any form by any means, graphic, electronic, or mechanical, including photocopy, recording, taping, or by any information storage or retrieval system, without permission in writing from the publisher, except in the case of reprints in the context of reviews, quotes, or references.

Scriptures marked NKJV are taken from the New King James Version®. Copyright © 1982 by Thomas Nelson. All rights reserved.

Printed in the United States of America

ISBN: 978-1-64484-585-1 (print)
ISBN: 978-1-64484-586-8 (ebook)

Special discounts are available on bulk quantity purchases by book clubs, associations and special interest groups. For details email: sales@publishyourgift.com or call **(888) 949-6228**. For information log on to www.PublishYourGift.com

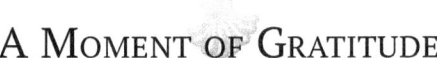

A Moment of Gratitude

To my first love, who is Jesus Christ. I thank you for this moment in time! You loved me before I truly loved myself. You have saved me from the plethora of bad decisions I have made and continue to make in my life. Thank you for going before me, being with me, never leaving me, and never forsaking me (Deuteronomy 31:6, NKJV) I do not ever desire to be anywhere without you so I pray that I always delight myself in you and you will give me the desires of my heart (Psalm 37:4, NKJV). I love you and praise your Holy name.

To my husband, Samuel. Thank you for your unwavering love, prayers, and support. I thank God that He created me for you. When I did not know what I needed, God knew and placed it in you when He formed you in your mother's womb. I love you, and I know the best is yet to come!

To my dearest and amazing mother, Mrs. Patricia A. May. Even in your struggles as a survivor of domestic violence, you always ensured you showered my siblings and me with unconditional love. When you were given an easy opportunity to leave us with our grandmother to be raised and go on with your life after your divorce to our father, you, at the age of twenty-eight, chose to make the hard choice and raise us yourself. Many would not understand why I state the 'easy opportunity' and the 'hard choice,' so please allow me to explain. My mother was a homemaker raising three children who was in love with my father. She also knew that if she stayed in the home, she probably would not be here with us today. She had no credit established but she knew her source, God. She knew that her children and she would be better together, and she knew that she could do anything as long as she trusted God. It was very common for grandparents to raise their grandchildren, which is why I said an easy opportunity. Instead, my mom would start working part-time at a grocery store then working her way to full-time employment with benefits. She would then apply for a sectional sofa as her first line of credit. I still remember that beautiful light gray sectional. Within a few years of discipline and being a faithful tither, she would apply and be approved to build her own three-bedroom, two-bathroom home. Then—yes there is more—two months after moving into our new home, my mom drove off the car lot with a brand new Mercury Topaz. I am still in awe and gratitude to how God blessed us and that was more than thirty years ago. There was never a day that we were without because God continues to provide.

Please do not hear what I am not saying. There would be times I was supposed to be asleep, but I would hear my mom in her bedroom crying. All I could do was pray for her on the other side of her bedroom door that God would hear her cries and comfort her the way I know He can. As many years would pass and I am in my adult life, I was faced with hardship and the fear of divorcing my former husband of eleven years, I reminded myself that if my mom could do it with three children, I can most definitely do it with none. I had no excuse if I truly wanted to live with peace of mind and happiness. All I had to do was take the first step and trust that God would meet me there and guide me to the next ones. He did just that. Momma, I love you so much and I praise Abba Father for blessing me with one of the most caring, gentle, and strong women on this Earth to be birthed by and to raise me into the woman I am today. You are a joy to know and call Momma.

To the women out there, for all your stressors, struggles, and strains, know that you are not alone. I pray that my book encourages you to keep fighting the good fight of faith and always remember to P.U.S.S.H.H. (Pray until something supernatural happens, honey). I love you, my Queen Sister.

TABLE OF CONTENTS

Introduction ... 1

Chapter 1: You Are a Child of God ... 5

Chapter 2: You Are a Queen ... 23

Chapter 3: You Are a Friend ... 35

Chapter 4: You Are a Mother ... 49

Chapter 5: You Are a Sister ... 65

About the Author ... 81

Introduction

The Bible tells us in Romans 8:18 (NKJV): "For I consider that the sufferings of this present time are not worthy to be compared with the glory which shall be revealed in us." This is why I felt it was imperative that I write this book. We do not have to look, feel, or walk like what we have been through. Many of us have just come out of a 'storm' and it seems like another one is on the horizon. Or maybe we just entered into it. Well, as my beloved pastor, Dr. James E. Williams, says, we do not have to look like what we are going through.

For me, I have many chapters in my "life" novel, from growing up in a single-parent home to becoming a survivor of different levels of abuse to infertility. I would be remiss if I did not mention that I am a beautiful Black woman, serving in the armed forces. I have been discriminated against more than I care to allow my mind to recall because I realize love and hate cannot occupy in my heart at the same time. My constant prayer to God is not allow my heart to harden by the sufferings that I face or those connected to me may face. I want to love like Jesus Christ loves. This is not an easy journey, however; but it has given me the wisdom, strength, and faith that God is able.

Celebrate your achievements! Fast from negativity! Refrain from speaking negative things, nor allowing negative thoughts to stay in your head. I say that because they are going to come however, when they do, rebuke it. When the enemy tries to put those thoughts in your mind, speak over it! The Bible tells us in James 4:7 (NKJV): "Therefore submit to God. Resist the devil and he will flee from you." I want to bring your attention to the punctuation mark after the word God. It is a period—not a comma but a period. It is God saying this is most important: "Submit to Him." When we find ourselves in the hardest places in our lives, submit, or shall I say, trust in God. I get excited thinking about how God's grace and mercy covers us, especially in moments when we do not know how we are going to make it out of a situation. This is why prayer and meditation is so important in the body of Christ.

I have been journaling since the age of sixteen. As I became an adult, I focused more on the struggles I was going through in that current time. As I made it out of that 'storm' and into another one, I would capture it on the notepad with that date. To this day, when I am struggling with the current 'storm' of life, I would reference back to those old journals. I immediately reflect on what that 'storm' was and know that if God brought me out of that tsunami, I know without a doubt, I am coming out of this one victoriously. I make my declaration from reading and applying His word and I wait with expectancy.

Here is a nugget for you: When you pray and give the situation to God, do not go back later, and pick it back up. Trust Him with it.

This book is a part of my assignment from my Father in Heaven. He implanted it in my spirit with an urgency to release to you, His precious jewels. I have divided into the many facets of our lives, beginning with us being a child of His.

One of my spiritual brothers often says, "Woman of God, God give people for your life."

Therefore, in my devotional time, I went to the Bible and read Isaiah 43:4 (NKJV) and it says: "Since you were precious in My sight, you have been honored, and I have loved you; therefore, I will give men for you and people for your life." God is our loving, caring, sharing, Heavenly Father.

The Bible also tells us in Romans 15:4 (NKJV): "For whatever things were written before were written for our learning, that we through the patience and comfort of the scriptures might have hope." Throughout this book, I have provided you with daily scriptures as well as declarations to pray and meditate on that I believe will provide comfort and give you hope.

Remember, each day we have a choice. Each day that you awake, you have another opportunity. It is an opportunity to leave a legacy, for our children and our children's children. Make a choice each day to add to your legacy of how they will remember you as the amazing woman that you are.

CHAPTER 1

You Are a Child of God

As women, we are often subject to massive emotional and sometimes physical pain, be it from broken marriages, failure to achieve greater heights, bullying, limitations due to birth defects, domestic violence, or unloving kids. Through all of these troubles, we give ourselves fully. We devote ourselves to serving our children, our friends, or even our husbands. Most often, we forget that we need to be loved in return. We learn to live with the pain; we withdraw all our happiness for the happiness of others. However, what if we went back and wondered whether we deserve to be loved?

God is saying, "You are my child. And you are not alone in this." The Bible tells us in Jeremiah 1:5 (NKJV), "Before I formed you in the womb I knew you." God loves you just as you love your children. Think about how you stand with them even when they make mistakes. Think about how you love them unconditionally. Think about how you nurture them to be loveable members of the society. Think about how you never abandon them during their worst situations. In addition, when you think about those things, place yourself in their shoes with God as your parent and guardian.

See God as the Sovereign God who will never leave you, especially during your life struggles. Think about Him as the voice that whispers encouraging words when you feel down. When your marriage is on the verge of breaking, close your eyes and listen to God. For He will always be there, whispering, encouraging.

See God as that guardian who you can speak to whenever you get frustrated in life. He is that invisible encouragement that does not have to say a word. That shoulder that you lean on when tears are flowing endlessly. I can assure you, you will gather your strength once more. He will not have to speak. He will not have to do anything. He will only listen to your frustrations. In addition, he will nod in comprehension. Moreover, you will start smiling once again.

A child knows that she is safe whenever her parents are around; God is assuring you that you are His child and should feel safe in his presence. A child knows that her parents will have answers to all her complex questions about life so you should not worry about those questions you keep asking yourself:

Is it worth it?
Am I good enough?
Why am I undergoing all this?
Will my dreams ever come true?

As assuredly as a child dumps her complex questions upon her parents, why do we fail to ask our Father in Heaven? The Bible tells us in 1 John 5:14-15 (NKJV), "Now this is the confidence that we have in Him, that if we ask anything according to His will, He hears us. If we know that He hears us, whatever we ask, we know that we have the petitions that we have asked of Him." The same way you listen to your child, sometimes offering answers and sometimes waiting for the right time; why would God not listen the same way?

Remember Hannah, Elikannah's wife and the co-wife to Penninah. She unceasingly prayed, knelt before the altar, cried, asked God questions, wondered the reason that she was facing challenges. She even got to a point where she could not pray aloud anymore. Moreover, all Eli, the high priest, could see was the movement of her lips and thought she was drunk. Perhaps he may have been joking when he inquired why she was drunk so early. Perhaps he was serious.

Assuming he was serious, you can imagine the scene he saw which led to him telling Hannah she was drunk. She must have been emphasizing on her prayer. She must have been walking back and forth. She must have had tears flowing down her cheeks. She must have gotten to a point where she knelt down and raised her head towards heaven. She may even have shaken her head and her hair may have spread all over her face. She may have stood up and walked around again, praying earnestly. She may have acted like a possessed woman.

This scene may have shown a drunk woman, but guess what I see? A woman troubled in her spirit. One who is wondering why the world always acts upon her in what seems to be so harshly. With the challenges of her not conceiving. With the hurting words thrown at her by her husband's other wife. In those times, these were troubles enough, because for sure, she would not be considered Elikanah's unless she bore a son with him. She would barely inherit anything from him unless there was a son to claim the inheritance.

However, through all those troubling days, God was watching her. Up there in His heavenly throne, He must have silently said to Himself: "She is my daughter; I know what I placed in her but I need her to see how strong she is so others will see and know. I will bless her with a son whose deeds will be remembered and retold far and wide."

In your daily hustles, do you ever wonder "Why can I not get things done like others? Why am I suffering alone? Why am I always finding it hard to achieve while everyone else succeeds with very little effort?"

You are not alone, my beautiful Queen Sister. You have a Father—one who can do anything within a split second. In addition, He desires to see you work your way through hardships. Then right when you think it is over, just when you have almost given up, just when you are about to go insane with stresses, He appears. With a snap of a finger, that which you have always desired to receive appears at the palm of your hands. Just like that, you thrive!

We are children of God. We are going to suffer. I know this because in Romans 8:18 (NKJV): "For I consider that the sufferings of this present time are not worthy to be compared with the glory which shall be revealed in us." This is exciting to know, because regardless of what we may experience, we know that it has no comparison to what is just around the corner. Knowing this helps me to Praise God in the midst of the suffering. Even when it seems like there is consistent failures, setbacks, or loss. Our families or friends may be with constant troubles. Our dreams may be taking what seems to be too long and seem distant. Trust that God is always there. He always holds our hands. He always walks alongside us.

Sometimes He is silent, but He is there. Sometimes He will whisper encouraging words to you. Just listen for Him. Nevertheless, He is always there. When He sees that you are about to give up, He adds unto you hope. How does He do that you ask? It is with His word. The Bible says in Romans 15:4 (NKJV) that, "For whatever things were written before were written for our learning, that we through the patience and comfort of the scriptures might have hope." In His perfect and right time, He awes you with His blessings, with His gifts. So let me remind you again that Woman, you are a Child of God and because of that, you can have the confidence in knowing that He will always be present in every step and all things are possible when you believe in Him. I love you. However, God loves you more!

Daily Devotion:

"His delight is in the law of the Lord, and in His law he [this includes us my queen sisters] meditates day and night."

—Psalm 1:2 (NKJV)

Day One:

Hebrews 11:1 (NKJV)

Now faith is the substance of things hoped for, the evidence of things not seen.

DECLARATION:

If God said it, that settles it! I will keep my faith in Him.

Day Two:

PHILIPPIANS 4:13 (NKJV)

I can do all things through Christ who strengthens me.

DECLARATION:

THERE IS NO THING THAT I CANNOT DO WHEN CHRIST IS IN, THROUGH, AND WITH ME.

Day Three:

Psalm 34:1 (NKJV)

I will bless the Lord at all times; His praise shall continually be in my mouth.

DECLARATION:

Regardless of what I may face on today, I will continue to praise the Lord.

Day Four:

GENESIS 1:26 (NKJV)

So God created man in His own image; in the image of God He created him; male and female He created them.

DECLARATION:

I ACCEPT EVERYTHING ABOUT MYSELF BECAUSE GOD CREATED ME IN HIS OWN IMAGE.

Day Five:

PSALM 82:6 (NKJV)

You are gods, and all of you are children of the Most High.

DECLARATION:

I WILL NOT HOLD BACK FROM BELIEVING THAT I AM A CHILD OF GOD.

Day Six:

PSALM 24:1 (NKJV)

*The earth is the Lord's and all its fullness:
the world, and those who dwell therein.*

DECLARATION:

AS I GO ABOUT MY DAY, I WILL PAY CLOSER ATTENTION TO THE FULLNESS OF THE EARTH, KNOWING THAT IT BELONGS TO GOD.

Day Seven:

1 John 3:1-2 (NKJV)

Behold, what manner of love the Father has bestowed on us, that we should be called children of God! Therefore, the world does not know us, because it did not know Him.

DECLARATION:

I WILL DEMONSTRATE MY GRATITUDE TO MY FATHER IN HEAVEN.

CHAPTER 2

You Are a Queen

When I think about women, I imagine the difficulties we undergo. And yet, when we are amongst everyone else, we put our best face, and putting everything troubling us aside just so we can fulfill our duties. What title would you give such a person if not that which is worthy of the highest rank in a kingdom? When we think of a queen, we see a woman who has privileges in huge amounts. I am sure we are right. Why else do we enjoy being showered as queens?

A queen has multiple handmaids who look after her so she can be beautiful whenever she appears before the people. They also look after her household; clean her living areas, change her linen and launder her clothes, and prepare the meals and dinner table. Therefore, the queen can focus on matters of kingdom's importance: the palace, the king, the community, and her children.

All these privileges, God has promised us when we join Him and His Son Jesus in Heaven where He rules. Sometimes I think about Heaven and the enjoyment that will be there, with no stress or struggles. We do not have to do all those things that prevent us from focusing on matters that are fundamental to our existence. In Heaven, we will exist to worship and praise our loving, caring, sharing, Heavenly Father.

Still, I remind myself that we are queens here on Earth. For it is where we live, and it is where we undergo problems. It is on Earth that we wonder sometimes why we exist in the first place. The Bible tells us in Isaiah 43:7 (NKJV): "Everyone who is called by my name, whom I have created for my glory, I have formed him, yes, I have made him."

When I was a little girl, I liked to think about myself as a princess and would always carry myself as books and movies depicted princesses. Back then, I never wanted to imagine what real life would look like or connect it to being a princess. I used to act it out as I thought a princess should. My parents even treated me like a princess. If I followed logic, a princess grows up to be a queen.

Besides that, I would like to think about the power that God has afforded every woman, despite the struggles we face. A power that equals—yet sometimes would even surpass—that of a queen. A queen is stressed by the ups and downs of the palace court, and when ruling alongside the king, she is faced with the struggles of being a wife and a queen simultaneously. Remember that whatever it is that you do, God has placed queen-like traits in each of us. There is a power that we as women always have. That feminine power enables us to rise above every circumstance and tribulation.

It is the power to manage everything around us properly, with God's help of course. Think about a queen who controls the whole kingdom, rules the palace court with an iron fist while showing her normal Godly-given tenderness towards her subordinates. Think about yourself in your field of expertise.

Perhaps you are a stay-at-home mom. Think about how you maintain your household with such grace that every member of your family, including your husband, reverences your diligence and queendom role.

Perhaps you are a manager at your organization. Think about how you ensure your colleagues listen to you without being commanding.

Likewise, how you treat your subordinates with unwavering tenderness that ensures they listen and obey you out of love. Can you not see the qualities of a queen in yourself? Do you not see the power that comes with only being a woman?

Perhaps you are nurse or a doctor. Do you ever stop to consider the power you have over your patients—a miraculous power like that possessed by Christ? I think that patients receive healing, as Jesus said, out of their faith in Him and through you, my Queen Sister. They have brought their faith to you, hoping that their physical, mental, or even emotional troubles will go away.

Do you ever think of Esther, the famous Jew who glowed through the power shown on her by our Almighty God, such that when the Persian King witnessed it, he could not resist her beauty? Esther did not come from nobility, nor was she brought up to become a queen. Nevertheless, there was something irresistible about her that not even the other young women could match. Perhaps it was because the Holy Spirit dwelling within her. Perhaps it was because she was chosen to save the people of Israel in time of troubles. Overall, she became the wife of a King who defied Jews.

Yet, she was a normal woman, like you and me. When she became Queen, she did what was uncustomary, an act that would guarantee her a death penalty: she approached the King without invitation, after she learned that Haman was planning to execute her people. It must have taken a lot of courage for her to do so, a belief in herself that was immeasurable. Moreover, out of her confidence, it resulted in the King ordering Haman's execution instead.

In the face of anxieties, when you make decisions in order to protect the wellbeing of your family, I see you, my Queen Sister. I can picture how you will act. I can see you mustering courage, believing in your abilities, and running towards danger. I see you risking your safety, even your life, to maintain the survival of your family. You do it for the people that you love and care for. So, believe me when I say that you are a queen. You are a woman that has sharp, painful arrows, knives, even axes piercing your back while from the front, you keep a smile and brighten everyone else's day. I see you! I appreciate you! I adore you! I love you, Queen!

Day Eight:

Psalm 139:14 (NKJV)

I will praise You; for I am fearfully and wonderfully made: marvelous are Your works; and that my soul knows very well.

DECLARATION:

I WILL PONDER ON HOW AMAZING GOD CREATED ME. A BEAUTIFUL QUEEN SISTER.

Day Nine:

Psalm 23:1 (NKJV)

*The Lord is my shepherd;
I shall not want.*

DECLARATION:

I have everything I need in the Lord.

Day Ten:

MATTHEW 6:9-13 (NKJV)

Our Father in Heaven, hallowed be Your name. Your kingdom come, Your will be done, on earth as it is in heaven. Give us this day our daily bread. And forgive us our debts, As we forgive our debtors. And do not lead us into temptation, but deliver us from the evil one. For Yours is the kingdom and the power and the glory forever. Amen.

DECLARATION:

I WILL ALWAYS ACKNOWLEDGE AND PRAISE MY FATHER IN HEAVEN THROUGHOUT EACH DAY OF MY LIFE.

Day Eleven:

Psalm 92:1-2 (NKJV)

It is good to give thanks to the Lord, and to sing praises to Your name, O Most High. To declare Your loving kindness in the mornings, and Your faithfulness every night.

DECLARATION:

I am thankful for so many things that God has done on today.

Day Twelve:

1 John 4:8 (NKJV)

*He who does not love does not know God,
for God is love.*

DECLARATION:

I will reflect and be grateful of the beauty of God's unwavering love for me.

Day Thirteen:

PSALM 37:25 (NKJV)

I have been young and now am old; yet I have never seen the righteous forsaken, nor his descendants begging bread.

DECLARATION:

WHEN I CONSIDER MY JOURNEY AND HOW FAR GOD HE HAS BROUGHT ME, I KNOW IT IS MORE THAN ENOUGH REASON TO GIVE HIM PRAISE.

Day Fourteen:

Psalm 102:1 (NKJV)

Hear my prayer, O Lord, and let my cry come to you.

DECLARATION:

I know that God hears my cry, and I am grateful for that.

CHAPTER 3

YOU ARE A FRIEND

I tend to think that between men and women, women maintain relationships for longer periods and fight to keep them positive. In fact, a study conducted by Laura Klein and Shelley Taylor showed that women are hardwired for friendships such that when things get hard, they seek out the company of fellow women and sometimes anyone who is close to them.

When I reflect upon my life, I realize that there have been multiple instances when I was frustrated with life, when what I desired was not coming to me no matter how hard I worked or how earnestly I prayed. I realize too that there have been instances when I was feeling unimportant. There have been instances when all I wanted to do was cry—and that is just what I did. There were even instances when life only threw curve balls or fastballs at me. In all of these instances, my circle of friends would come to my aid. Whether it was just to be a listening ear or provide sound advice, they were there. What each of them provided was something you are unable to put a price tag on. Their friendship, their companionship, and their shoulder they placed under me so I could cry my eyes dry. The type of friends who would lend a listening ear and their constant reminders to own the space that I may be in, whether it is good or bad, yet reassuring me that it will not always be like this. Praying for you as much as you pray for each of them. Would there be anything as invaluable as that?

Upon reflection too, we realize that we have not been alone in these womanly troubles. Others have been facing difficulties in life. Parenting proving difficult, some experiencing their husbands becoming difficult as well, or a boss who does not treat women with respect, an economic situation that may lead to house evacuation, or a disease that that has been troubling her or a member of her family.

Whatever the circumstance may be, know that you have friends that will be there to lend a shoulder to cry on. At the same token, be the friend that will lend her shoulder for another as well. Each time my husband and I relocate to another state due to change in our duty station, I always rely back on my constant and solid friends. I go into the new location with the mindset that I have reached my capacity in friends. I am here to do an assignment not here to establish friendships however, if I gain friends in the process, I view it as a bonus from God. I will say, there has not been a duty station we have served at that I have not crossed paths and gains not just friends but sisters. My best friend Nicky C. and I met in Seoul, South Korea, in 2013. When I walked into the office, she immediately jumped up out of her seat and came to the door to greet me. "Finally, another woman here to help balance out the testosterone within the office," she said as I looked around and saw two other females in the room. I replied, "Okay," as I looked at her rather strangely. She and I laugh about this encounter to this day, and I am certain she is going to scream my name when she learns that you all now know all about it too.

We became best of friends, and would you believe when it was time to change duty stations, we both received assignments to Fort Bragg, North Carolina? We served in the same company as a matter of a fact. It does not stop there. Few years later, it was time to change duty stations again and yes, we both received assignments to Hawaii. I must tell you that neither of us planned this. This was God's entire and perfect plan. During this period, we both experienced major life changing events such as hard divorces, pregnancy loss, and the loss of close family members. We also experienced the discovery of new love, marriage, major career progressions, and birth of beautiful life.

I recall hearing the Bible story about Mary and her cousin Elizabeth. The angel Gabriel gives Mary a word from the Lord that she will bring forth a son named Jesus. He also shares with her that her cousin Elizabeth, a woman in age, was also with child. She was six months pregnant at the time. Mary goes to visit Elizabeth and upon hearing Mary's voice, Elizabeth's baby leaped in her womb, and she was filled with the Holy Spirit. A mentor said to look for people that make your spirit leap because they are connected to your destiny. Immediately I thought of the initial encounter with Nicky and began to praise God for blessing me with such an amazing friend.

I am certain you have similar experiences as well. You may not entirely know the impact your presence meant to a person at the time. How appreciative they were to you for hugging them tightly and assuring them that everything is going to be okay. I do believe they felt the way you did when they also stood by you during your hard times.

Continue being that great friend. Make love deposits rather than withdrawals. Take the time to show your gratitude to those who matter in your life. You are a wonderful woman and friend. I am certain that there is someone in need of a friend like you. Embrace the journey because your presence in this world is not in vain, for someone will need you to be there for them. It could be your husband. It could be your little brother. It could be your sister. It could be your mother. Most importantly, it could be a stranger. God created you for a purpose.

In the same manner that you would need a friend to be there for you, to remind you of the positive and beautiful things you possess, you, being a woman will be there for someone. Sometimes it does not even require that person to be a relative of yours. Sometimes just being a woman means that we are there to offer smiles, helping hands, inspirational messages, encouraging words, our shoulders to lean on, and even just our very presence. That is my hope with this book: that you know that I genuinely care for each of you. I do not need to know you in order for me to love and care for you.

Whenever you feel like you are not important or you wonder what your role is, I hope you think about the essence of just being a woman and you will feel worthy again. In the story of creation, God created everything that was good and beautiful and when He stepped back and observed from a distance, He was pleased with Himself. He had even created man, one who had His own image and likeness and had given him authority over the rest of His creation. After a while, the Bible says in Genesis 2:18 (NKJV), "And the Lord God said, 'It is not good that man should be alone; I will make him a helper comparable to him.'" How amazing and loving our God is that He saw that Man would need a helpmeet. God placed Adam into a deep sleep, took one of his ribs, and created Woman. In Genesis 2:23, Adam said, "This is now bone of my bones and flesh of my flesh; she shall be called woman because she was taken out of man. God could have created anything to be the companion of Man and yet, He chose a Woman. God formed us with the ability to be a source of life, of happiness, and of company to our amazing kings.

You are a woman, and being a friend is your most valuable quality.

Day Fifteen:

PROVERBS 18:24 (NKJV)

A man who has friends must himself be friendly, but there is a friend who sticks closer than a brother.

DECLARATION:

I WILL BEGIN SHARING THINGS WITH JESUS BEFORE I SHARE IT WITH MY BEST FRIEND.

Day Sixteen:

1 THESSALONIANS 5:11 (NKJV)

Therefore, comfort each other and edify one another, just as you also are doing.

DECLARATION:

I WILL MAKE A MORE DELIBERATE EFFORT IN GIVING MY FRIENDS MY UNINTERRUPTED ATTENTION. THEY DESERVE IT.

Day Seventeen:

Colossians 3:12-14 (NKJV)

Therefore, as the elect of God, holy and beloved, put on tender mercies, kindness, humility, meekness, longsuffering, bearing with one another, and forgiving one another. If anyone has a complaint against another; even as Christ forgave you, so you also must do.

DECLARATION:

I WILL FORGIVE ALL HAS HURT ME.

Day Eighteen:

1 Cor. 15:33 (NKJV)

Do not be deceived: Evil company corrupts good habits.

DECLARATION:

TAKE SOME TIME TO DO SELF-EXAMINATION OF WHAT I AM PUTTING OUT INTO RELATIONSHIPS.

Day Nineteen:

ECCLESIASTES 4:10 (NKJV)

For if they fall, one will lift up his companion, but woe to him who is alone when he falls, for he has no one to help him up.

DECLARATION:

I AM GRATEFUL FOR THE PEOPLE I CAN RELY ON.

Day Twenty:

Proverbs 16:20 (NKJV)

He who heeds the word wisely will find good, and whoever trusts in the Lord, happy is he.

DECLARATION:

Regardless of my circumstances, I am happy because I trust in the Lord.

Day Twenty-One:

PHILIPPIANS 4:4 (NKJV)

Rejoice in the Lord always. Again I will say, rejoice!

DECLARATION:

REGARDLESS OF MY NEW CIRCUMSTANCES, I WILL REJOICE IN THE LORD BECAUSE I STILL TRUST IN HIM.

CHAPTER 4

YOU ARE A MOTHER

You would never think of yourself as a woman without remembering the lessons you learned from your mother—sometimes through observation and direction, and sometimes through warnings.

I tend to remember my mother mostly out of things I observed as a young girl. My mother used to take some time after serving us dinner and seeing us to our bedrooms to read one of her books. She would tell me sometimes that she wanted to be a better mom by keeping her mental health intact. In the mornings, she would look to ensure that we looked smart, that we did not go to school with empty stomachs, and that we observed table manners. On weekends, she would ensure that after completing our assignments we played and enjoyed the weekend like any other kid. She did this while keeping a watchful eye on us. Ensuring that we did not behave in the manner we were not supposed to. She ensured we grew up to be the people we are today.

On Sunday mornings, she prepared us for church and ensured that we followed what the pastor said. I remember that she often referred to a sermon every time we behaved contrary to her teachings.

What awes me to this day is the fact that my mother never complained about any problems. Was she perfect, I wonder? Did not she undergo challenges that I undergo now? Moreover, when I asked her once, she told me, "That is what it means to be a mother."

Think about the challenges of being a mother—a woman in general, for that matter—and you will realize your strength is beyond measure. Do you ever look at your children and see how much faith they have in you? Do you ever wonder why they always seek your counsel, and most often your encouragement? Do you ever look at them, their behavior, their decision-making, even how they relate with others, and ask yourself, "This is my doing?" Well, I think you should. I applaud you for your strength and being the best mother that you are!

I met a mom once. Her daughter received a diagnosis of autism spectrum disorder in her early infancy. As she told me her story, I could not prevent my tears from flowing and she, the one who had undergone the struggles of keeping her child healthy socially and emotionally, was providing me with tissues. She described how they realized that their daughter was gazing at one point and never even took note of them. She told me how they went through one doctor after another trying to counter the disorder attempt to treat the baby. She told me how they had to design ways in which they would cope with their daughter. She narrated how it was so difficult to get her to school. How she would run back to her when she dropped her at the gate. How sometimes the teachers had to close the gate to keep her in school. How she felt that she had no friends. How she explained it to her mother, and she tried to comfort her. How they tried to keep her among people so she could get used to them. And how she was afraid that they both might not be there during her adulthood, and she may lack the support she so much deserves.

Yet, the mom was smiling all the way. Telling me how hard it had been, but that it was worth it. For now, she feels proud that she did not give up. Many of you may not have given birth to children yet like me. That does not mean that you are not a mother. You may be a bonus mother, as I have been given the most amazing pleasure of being to two amazing women, Kyra and Kimani.

Maybe you are not a bonus mother, but I would like to think about your siblings or cousins even. Think how you helped bring up your little brother or sister. Think about looking after your elderly father or mother. Think about looking after your husband. Think about being there for your co-workers, for your friends, and even for their children. Think about these things and you will be proud that you are a mother.

I often think about the story of Hagar, and I realize that being a mother is not easy, and yet it defines a woman and her strength. Many of you may ask why I am not mentioning the story of Sarah. Well, I would like to give you a different perspective. First, Abraham had been given a word from the Lord that he took back to his wife Sarah however, she had alternate plans. Hagar was Sarah's handmaid and when it seemed clear that Sarah would not bear a child with Abraham, she offered Hagar to him. They argued and Sarah convinced Abraham that he needed an heir and with Sarah being "caught up" with her worldly knowledge that "she was too old to bear children," this seemed logical to her to give her maidservant to her husband. So, for the family of her masters, Hagar became pregnant. Sarah hated Hagar so much for the ease of bearing children and she treated her harshly to the extent that Hagar fled. She roamed the wilderness until she was out of water. Yet, the Lord commanded her to go back to Sarah, to give birth and bring up a son Ishmael in the house from which she had run away. She had to oblige. All Hagar was doing was obeying Sarah's request. I am sure she did not want to be with Abraham, yet Hagar did what Sarah told her to do which was to bring what she thought would be joy and satisfaction to Sarah. We all see how that turned out though. How many of us have done things for those we care about, besides our own thoughts and feelings on the matter, just to end up being viewed as the bad person?

Do you ever think of the pride Mary must have had for being Christ's mother? Can you imagine the pain she must have felt when she saw His rejection by the people who He had healed, taught, even raised from the dead? Yet, at one point Jesus had told Mary, when she sent for him as he taught a congregation, that His family consisted only of those people who were listening to and following Him. The same people rejected her son. She was helpless and all she could do was weep, and perhaps tend to his grave.

Coping with such kind of pain is what it means to be a mother. Being a mother is part of what being a woman is. I recall my mom always displaying such strength to us, and I guess that is because society has socialized women to always be strong. But I'm here to say that there is nothing wrong with being transparent to God, your trusted friends, and mostly yourself. It is okay to be vulnerable. It is okay to cry out when you need to because God created our tear ducts for that very reason.

To my beautiful Queen Sisters who are struggling to conceive, you are not alone. About eleven years ago, I learned that I have polycystic ovary syndrome (PCOS) after many unsuccessful attempts to conceive. Giving birth to children is my greatest desire, and as the years went by, I became more and more anxious because I was focused on my worldly knowledge that my egg reserve will be depleted by age forty. Well, just before my forty-second birthday, my husband and I began our in-vitro fertilization (IVF) journey. The doctor retrieved forty eggs from my ovaries. The enemy began to whisper in my ear, "Well, you may have forty eggs, but they are not viable." How many of you know that the devil is a liar? Thirty-six of those forty eggs were mature, viable eggs. We had twenty-three that fertilized, and then after pre-implantation genetic testing (PGT), God blessed us with eleven beautiful day-five blastocysts. My story does not end there. We have experienced two pregnancy losses since then, and I will tell you, it is difficult. However, when you know whom you belong to and what He has promised you, it gives you the strength to keep holding on. I am not relying on my worldly knowledge, but my heart knowledge of the signs, wonders, and miracles my Father in Heaven has done and continues to do.

I have a close sister friend, Sonoma M., who was told in the beginning of her adult years that she would not be able to bear children due to her severe endometriosis. She not only has three beautiful daughters to whom I am an auntie, but she is carrying her fourth child now. God is so awesome, and I remind myself, as I genuinely rejoice with her, that if God can do it for her, He will do it for me. So, I say again, stay encouraged, keep your faith in God, and trust that He has it all figured out. Do not let your doubting hands pull up the seed you planted with faith hands.

Day Twenty-Two:

PSALM 127:3 (NKJV)

Behold, children are a heritage from the Lord, the fruit of the womb is a reward.

DECLARATION:

I WILL DEMONSTRATE MY GRATITUDE TO THE LORD FOR MY WONDERFUL REWARD.

Day Twenty-Three:

Song of Solomon 7:5 (NKJV)

Your head crowns you like Mount Carmel, and the hair of your head is like purple; a king is held captive by your tresses.

DECLARATION:

I WILL BASK IN THE FULL BEAUTY OF WHO I AM.

Day Twenty-Four:

ROMANS 12:10 (NKJV)

Be kindly affectionate to one another with brotherly love, in honor giving preference to one another, not lagging in diligence, fervent in spirit, serving the Lord.

DECLARATION:

LORD, I JUST WANT TO SAY THANK YOU FOR THE PLANS YOU HAVE FOR MY LIFE.

Day Twenty-Five:

John 14:27 (NKJV)

Peace I leave with you, My peace I give to you, not as the world gives do I give to you. Let not your heart be troubled, neither let it be afraid.

DECLARATION:

How awesome of a feeling is it to know that Jesus gave His perfect peace to always comfort me?

Day Twenty-Six:

1 Cor. 15:57 (NKJV)

But thanks be to God, who gives us the victory through our Lord Jesus Christ.

DECLARATION:

I AM VICTORIOUS BECAUSE I HAVE JESUS CHRIST.

Day Twenty-Seven:

Isaiah 54:13 (NKJV)

All your children shall be taught by the Lord, and great shall be the peace of your children.

DECLARATION:

Beginning today, I will teach my children about our Lord and Savior Jesus Christ.

Day Twenty-Eight:

Proverbs 22:6 (NKJV)

Train up a child in the way he should go, and when he is old he will not depart from it.

DECLARATION:

Celebrate you each day for being a loving, caring and devoted mother.

CHAPTER 5

YOU ARE A SISTER

We know that we were all created differently and in God's image. It is because of that fact that we are beautiful. The Bible tells us in Psalms 139:14 (NKJV), "I will praise you, for I am fearfully and wonderfully made; marvelous are your works and that my soul knows very well." The word wonderfully derives from the root word wonderful, which means inspiring delight, pleasure, or admiration—extremely good. You are my sister and I believe in everything you believe you are, according to how God created us to be.

Oftentimes, we as women, fail to uplift and encourage another woman, whether it be through compliments or even a genuine smile in passing. As if you didn't just see the beauty in her. Let us stop that, ladies. Let us change the culture that we have before us and acknowledge one another when we cross one another's paths. We do not know what our Queen Sister is going through. Know that there is nothing another woman has or receives from God that prevents you from receiving what God has planned for you. I recall in Jeremiah 29:11(NKJV) that God said, "He knows the plans he has for me, plans to prosper and not fail. Plans to give me hope and a future."

That is for each of us. His word does not have stipulations on it. That is not how it works. Rejoice with your Queen Sister genuinely. If my sister receives a promotion at work or builds her dream home first, guess what, I am beyond excited for both of them. Why? Because when one person wins, we all win! Rejoice with them because yours is not too far behind. God cannot reward you when you have jealousy and envy in your heart my beautiful Queen Sister, so let us start today with excitement and love for one another.

You are worthy and you are enough. Be overjoyed with you. Accept all things about you. Sure, there are things you may desire to change or enhance about yourself, but God does not make mistakes, so stop telling Him he messed up when you compare yourself to another Queen Sister. You may not realize it, but that is exactly what you are doing.

Invest and shine in your own life, then allow that peaceful light to shine on other women around you just the same. You would be surprised that the very woman you want to look like has insecurity about something too.

Can I share something personal with you? I had to stand before a wardrobe mirror in my nakedness and accept everything about me from my head to my toes. It was so difficult because I wanted lighter gums, curlier hair, a plump booty, and amazing smile like my sister. I was so focused on what was hers that I was not seeing what beauty that lies within me.

One day I said to her, you are so beautiful. She immediately said in shock, "Are you kidding me? You are so beautiful, Terrah. You are so gorgeous to me." I had no idea she saw me like that. I began to smile with my beautiful dark gums and embrace my gorgeous sister. Some of you may be battling with acceptance. Well, I say to you today: You are beautiful and so special! You are worthy of everything you desire. Starting today, you will make decisions that will fulfill the promises God has made to you. Walk in it! If you are not satisfied with your situation, change the atmosphere. Change is necessary for growth, new beginnings, and elevation. Some changes will be uncomfortable too.

Think about how many times you have awoken out of your sleep at night and went to the restroom. All of us have done it at some point in our lives. I think I wake up every night almost. Now imagine if I ask you to start doing lunges from your bed to the restroom each time you get up at night. First of all, you probably would say "Whatever, Terrah, I am not doing that." Your bladder is full, and you are sleepy, you may feel like you do not have time for that. However, if you began doing it, you will strengthen your core as well as your pelvic floor, even your quads and gluteus, if done properly. The benefits are great however changing and doing something you are not used to doing can be frustrating initially.

My husband and I have a plant that we received as a housewarming gift. After some time of watering it and giving it proper light, the plant began to grow bigger, so much so that was outgrowing the pot it was in. In order for it to continue flourishing and producing more leaves, we had to re-pot the plant into a larger flowerpot. We had to uproot the plant out of its current living space and place it into a new living space that was greater in size. Sometimes, in order for us to become who we desire to be, you must be willing to say goodbye to some of the old things we used to be. I understand that if it was as easy as reading the words in this book, you would have already made the necessary changes for whatever it is. Well, know that you are never alone in this journey of life. I have my daily struggles as well. Fears try to step in and consume my thoughts. I have to constantly remind myself that the Bible tells me in Philippians 4:8 (NKJV), "Finally, brethren, whatever things are true, whatever things are noble, whatever things are just, whatever things are pure, whatever things are lovely, whatever things are of good report, if there is any virtue and if there is anything praiseworthy—meditate on these things."

I know that the devil is the father of all lies and that my Father in Heaven cannot lie. So, whatever the enemy says, I stand on the word of God that had been implanted in my heart that helps me to overcome those fears. I realize that there is not enough room in my life for both fear and the belief that God will change my circumstance, in His perfect timing. God gave each of us a measure of faith and Hebrews 11:6 (NKJV) tells us that "without faith, it is impossible to please God." If it seems too hard to do on your own, that is because it is. Surrender it to God, trust Him to bring you out of it, and watch Him work.

One last thing I want to share with you, my Queen Sister, is this: You cannot control everything that will happen to you and around you, no matter how hard you may try. You do not know what is before you. Only God does. I say this to help you just relax and stop being so hard on yourself for "not seeing this coming." Your peace of mind and happiness is far greater. When the obstacles arise and you have a setback, know that it is okay! I will still be here, your friends will still be here, and most importantly, God will still be right here with you, right here in your corner, cheering you on to get back in the fight because we know that your victory is just a few steps away.

So, when I say you are a child of God, a queen, a friend, a mother, or a sister, smile broadly and nod with pride because Woman, you are!

I love you! I believe in you! God believes in you! I hope that you believe in you too!

Day Twenty-Nine:

Proverbs 19:20 (NKJV)

*Listen to counsel and receive instructions,
that you may be wise in your latter years.*

DECLARATION:

I WILL OPEN MYSELF UP TO LISTEN TO WISE COUNSEL AND INSTRUCTION IN ORDER TO BE A BETTER VERSION OF MYSELF.

Day Thirty:

NAHUM 1:7 (NKJV)

The Lord is good, a stronghold in the time of trouble; and He knows those who trust in Him.

DECLARATION:

I TRUST GOD WHOLEHEARTEDLY, REGARDLESS OF WHAT CIRCUMSTANCES COME MY WAY.

Day Thirty-One:

EPHESIANS 4:25 (NKJV)

Therefore, putting away lying, let each one of you speak truth with their neighbor, for we are members of one another.

DECLARATION:

STARTING TODAY, I WILL ONLY SPEAK LOVE IN TRUTH BECAUSE I LOVE MY BROTHERS AND SISTERS IN CHRIST.

Day Thirty-Two:

Luke 8:48 (NKJV)

And He said to her, "Daughter, be of good cheer, your faith has made you well. Go in peace."

DECLARATION:

My faith in Jesus Christ will not hinder me from being of good cheer.

Day Thirty-Three:

1 PETER 2:9 (NKJV)

But you are a chosen generation, a royal priesthood, a holy nation. His own special people, that you may proclaim the praises of Him who called you out of darkness into His marvelous light.

DECLARATION:

I AM ROYALTY!

Day Thirty-Four:

JOHN 15:14 (NKJV)

Jesus said, "You are my friends if you do whatever I command you."

DECLARATION:

I AM SO GRATEFUL THAT I HAVE A TRUE FRIEND IN JESUS CHRIST. HE IS GRACIOUS, LOVING AND ALWAYS DEPENDABLE.

Day Thirty-Five:

Revelation 2:4 (NKJV)

Nevertheless, I have this against you, that you have left your first love.

DECLARATION:

STARTING TODAY, I WILL NOT ALLOW ANY CIRCUMSTANCE TO KEEP ME FROM MY FIRST LOVE, JESUS CHRIST.

My Prayer for You

Most gracious Father in Heaven, I come into Your presence with a thankful heart. You made it possible for me to write this book while ensuring that my sister would read it. I pray that she finds life, hope, strength, joy, and peace in it. Thank you, Father God. You are able to do exceedingly and abundantly, above all we can ask or think.

Father God, we invite you into our hearts. Examine us through and through; find everything that hides within each of us. Put us to the test and sift through all of our anxious cares, for Your word tells us to be anxious for nothing, but in prayer and supplication, with thanksgiving, we let our request be made known, and the peace of God that surpasses all of our understanding will guard our hearts and minds through Christ Jesus.

We rejoice in Your word. We place our faith in your word because we know there is nothing too hard for you. For without faith, it is impossible to please you, Lord. Stir up the gifts and talents you have placed in each of us. I bind up the oppression, suppression and depression in the name of Jesus. We shall live and not die. I thank you that You would not withhold any good thing from us.

Give my sister the strength she needs to change whatever situation or circumstance that you say needs to be changed. Remove anything and anyone from her life that prevents you from using her in the manner that you created her. It is all for your glory, Lord. Open doors that no man can close, and I thank You for shutting doors that no man can open. Father God, Your understanding is beyond her comprehension. Help us to stop trying to figure out what you have already worked out. We give you all the glory, praise, and honor. May the words of my mouth and the mediation of my heart be acceptable in your sight, Father God, for You are our strength and redeemer. It is in Your precious son Jesus's name we pray. Amen.

About the Author

Terrah S. Bell is a writer, podcaster, member of the armed forces, and, most importantly, a woman of God. Inspired by the hardships of her mother, herself, and the many women around her, Terrah wrote Woman, You Are: A 30-Day Devotional for Prayer and Meditation to empower, encourage, and uplift women who may have forgotten how important and loved they are by God.

Terrah published her first short story, "Ruby Red," in October 2021 while launching her podcast, Queendom Talks with Terrah, which empowers and inspires women of color to stand in the face of adversity and become the strong women they were meant to be.

Terrah and her husband, Samuel Bell, reside in Ewa Beach, Hawaii. They are active members of Life More Abundantly Island Church under the leadership of Pastors, Dr. James E. Williams and Dr. Gigi Williams. She has two bonus daughters, Kyra Bell and Kimani Felder. Terrah has two brothers, Harriel and Terry; two sisters, Vanessa and Patricia; and five nieces and nephews, Alyssa, Tericia, Coby, CJ, and Pasleigh.

    Follow her on Instagram @queendomtalkswithterrah

CREATING DISTINCTIVE BOOKS
WITH INTENTIONAL RESULTS

We're a collaborative group of creative masterminds with a mission to produce high-quality books to position you for monumental success in the marketplace.

Our professional team of writers, editors, designers, and marketing strategists work closely together to ensure that every detail of your book is a clear representation of the message in your writing.

Want to know more?
Write to us at info@publishyourgift.com
or call (888) 949-6228

Discover great books, exclusive offers, and more at
www.PublishYourGift.com

Connect with us on social media

@publishyourgift

www.ingramcontent.com/pod-product-compliance
Lightning Source LLC
Chambersburg PA
CBHW071909070526
44583CB00016B/1910